NOW THAT'S INTERESTING

KENTUCKY'S CAPITOL

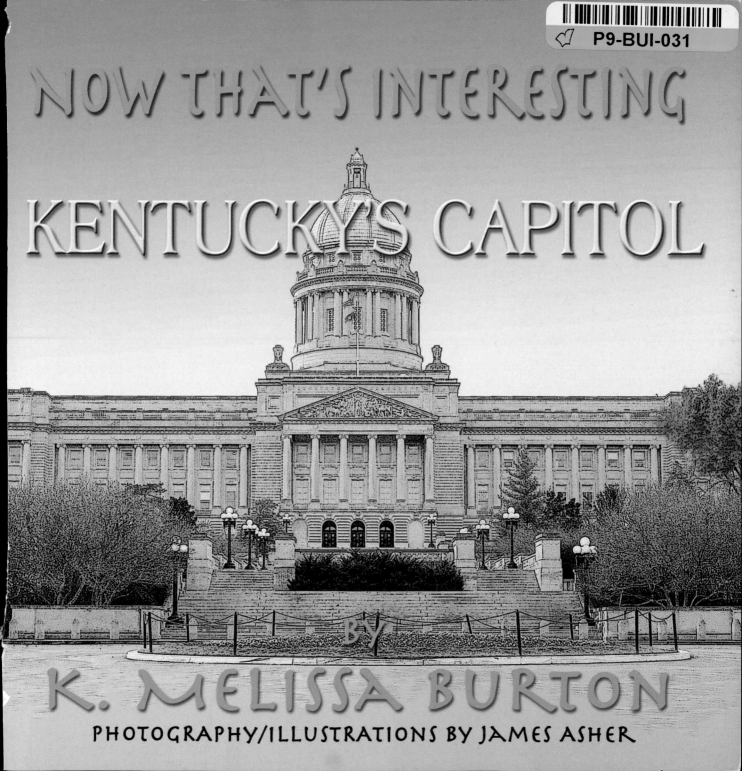

BY

K. MELISSA BURTON

PHOTOGRAPHY/ILLUSTRATIONS BY JAMES ASHER

International Standard Book Number 978-0-913383-96-4
Library of Congress Card Catalog Number 2007921548

Cover design and book layout by Asher Graphics
Photos/Illustrations by James Asher unless otherwise credited below

Manufactured in the United States of America

All book order correspondence should be addressed to:

McClanahan Publishing House, Inc.
P.O. Box 100
Kuttawa, KY 42055

270-388-9388
800-544-6959
270-388-6186 FAX

www.kybooks.com

Page 5—Photo of capitol with flowers courtesy of the Kentucky Department of Libraries and Archives, Frankfort, Kentucky.
Page 7—Photo of floral clock courtesy of the Kentucky Department of Libraries and Archives, Frankfort, Kentucky.
Page 8—Map courtesy of the Kentucky Historical Society, Frankfort, Kentucky.
Page 9—Line cuts of the first and second Capitol Buildings courtesy of the Kentucky Historical Society, Frankfort, Kentucky.
Pages 10 and 11—Photos of the Old Capitol Building taken with permission from the Kentucky Historical Society, Frankfort, Kentucky.
Page 18—Photo of Capitol under construction courtesy of the Kentucky Department of Libraries and Archives, Frankfort, Kentucky.
Page 29—Photo of the State Reception Room courtesy of the Kentucky Department of Libraries and Archives, Frankfort, Kentucky.

Foreword

You are one lucky kid! Kentucky is an incredible state. Whether you're from Kentucky, visiting, or just looking for information, Kentucky is a place loaded with interesting people and beautiful places. It's also full of history—not the kind that makes you take a nap but the kind that involves murder, mysteries, and colorful personalities.

Growing up in Kentucky, I was able to visit several of the fascinating landmarks that help make Kentucky special. Even now I remember a third grade field trip to Fort Harrod where I sat in Kentucky's first school building, and I can't count the times I've driven through Frankfort and seen the capitol dome rising above the landscape.

As a teacher, I am honored to share some of Kentucky's "uncommon wealth" with my students, and now you, the reader. My hope is that in reading this book you will have gained a deeper understanding and appreciation of our great state. At the same time you'll be saying to yourself,   "Now that's interesting!"

Acknowledgements

Thank you to the wonderful tour guides at the Kentucky Capitol. Much of the information in this book came from them. A special thank you to Linda Stevens. Her insights have helped to make this book unique. Also, thank you to the people at the Kentucky Department of Libraries and Archives for their help locating historic photos. Aside from these sources, all other information in this book was gathered from a variety of Internet resources.

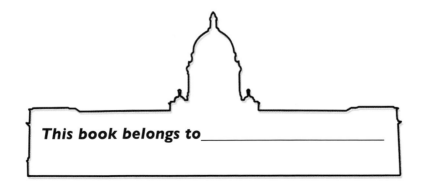

This book belongs to_____

On Capital Avenue in Frankfort, Kentucky stands one of the nation's most beautiful capitol buildings. Built from 1905-1909, the Kentucky Capitol Building is a proud landmark that belongs to every **citizen**, or person who lives within Kentucky. But before the current capitol was built, Kentucky had a long line of other capitols—some official and some unofficial.

NOW THAT'S INTERESTING!!!

The stone sculpture above the front doors of today's Capitol is called the Capitol Pediment. The woman at the center is Lady Kentucky. She is surrounded by "Progress," "Plenty," "Art," and "Agriculture."

The Gentleman from Kentucky

Kentucky's Capitol is full of history and beauty. It's not only the home for Kentucky's three branches of government; it's also a proud landmark for every citizen. Whether you're young or old, someone who votes or someone who does not, Kentucky's Capitol belongs to all its citizens. It's sure to be a Kentucky treasure both for now and many generations to come.

THE FLORAL CLOCK

Just behind the capitol is another feature that makes Kentucky's Capitol beautiful and unique. It's the Floral Clock. Members of the Garden Club of Kentucky dedicated this clock to Kentucky in 1961. With a face that is 34 feet wide, the clock will hold over 10,000 plants! It keeps time with the help of an electric motor that is hidden in the base of the clock. The clock does not make a gong or a ticking noise, but everyone is glad it does not have to be wound up.

The clock is partly surrounded by a pool and fountains. It's tradition in Kentucky to visit the clock, cast a coin in the pool and make a wish. When the pool has many coins, they are collected and the money is used to fund college scholarships for Kentucky students. One of those lucky students might be you!

FRANKFORT

THE CAPITAL 1871. OF KENTUCKY.

LOOKING SOUTH EAST

The drawing on this 1871 map shows the structure that leaders hoped would be the state's "new" capitol building. This new capitol was to be built on the same site as the 1830 capitol. However, the cost became too much and this proposed capitol was never constructed. A new building would have to wait until 1905.

KENTUCKY

Maysville

Ashland

Louisville

FRANKFORT

Lexington

Henderson

Owensboro

KENTUCKY
RIVER

Pikeville

Madisonville

Paducah

Bowling Green

Hopkinsville

After Daniel Boone founded Boonesborough in 1775, he and other representatives from other settlements met beneath a large elm tree in Danville, Kentucky. After nine tries, Virginia finally granted Kentucky statehood in 1792. For a short time, leaders of the new state met in a log cabin in what is now downtown Lexington. It was in this cabin that **Frankfort** was chosen to be the permanent capital of Kentucky. The town was not only centrally located but it was next to the Kentucky River which could offer both protection and transportation.

After Frankfort was chosen, state leaders met in a white-framed house until the first official capitol building was built in 1794. This building burned in 1813. Another capitol was built in 1814, but ten years later it also burned.

1794 capitol

1814 capitol

In an effort to stay away from wood, a stone building was built in 1830.

Gideon Shyrock was only 27 years old when he won the architecture contest for Kentucky's third capitol.

NOW
THAT'S INTERESTING!!!

The weight of the "floating staircase" rests upon a single stone. If this stone is moved even a fraction of an inch, the staircase will crumble.
Stray animals such as dogs, cows, and even hogs sometimes wandered onto the old capitol grounds until a fence was built in 1854.

The Gentleman
from Kentucky

OLD CAPITOL

GOVERNOR
WILLIAM GOEBEL

THE ABLE AND MOST EFFECTIVE ADVOCATE
AND CHAMPION OF THE PEOPLES CAUSE
THEIR LOVED AND LOYAL FRIEND.

ON JANUARY 30TH, 1900 HE WAS SHOT
DOWN BY AN ASSASSIN FROM THE PRIVATE
OFFICE OF THE THEN SECRETARY OF STATE.

BORN JANUARY 4TH, 1856
DIED FEBRUARY 3RD, 1900

"TELL MY FRIENDS TO BE
BRAVE AND FEARLESS AND LOYAL
TO THE GREAT COMMON PEOPLE"
HIS LAST WORDS.

WILLIAM GOEBEL

FELL HERE

JAN. 30TH, 1900

Today, you can still visit what Kentuckians have come to call the "Old" Capitol. It's the sight of the world's only "floating" staircase. It is also the place where governor-elect William Goebel was shot in 1900. Goebel died three days later and his death is still something of a mystery!

KENTUCKY STATE CAPITOL

FLOOR PLANS

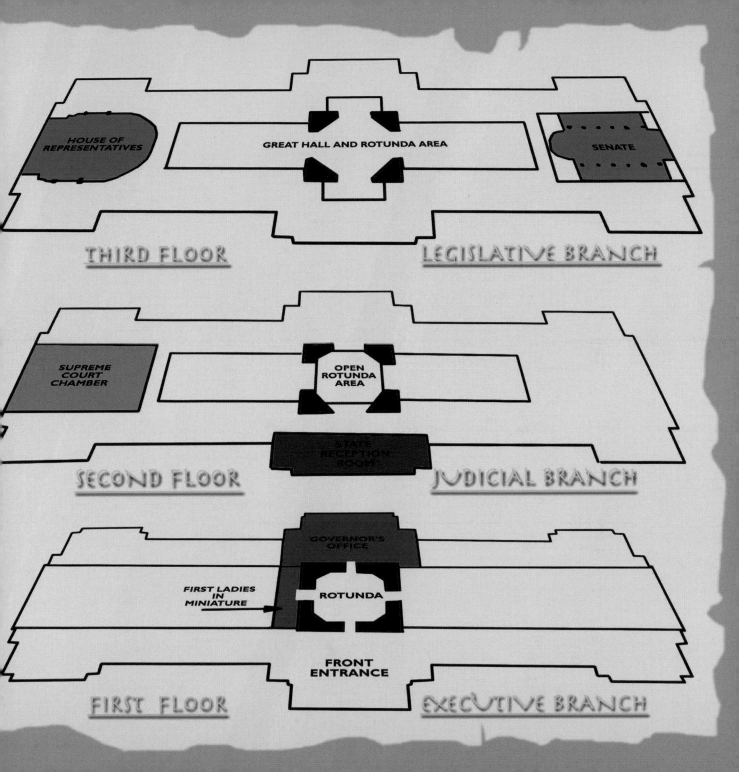

THIRD FLOOR — LEGISLATIVE BRANCH

HOUSE OF REPRESENTATIVES

GREAT HALL AND ROTUNDA AREA

SENATE

SECOND FLOOR — JUDICIAL BRANCH

SUPREME COURT CHAMBER

OPEN ROTUNDA AREA

STATE RECEPTION ROOM

FIRST FLOOR — EXECUTIVE BRANCH

GOVERNOR'S OFFICE

FIRST LADIES IN MINIATURE

ROTUNDA

FRONT ENTRANCE

ROTUNDA

Just inside the front door of the capitol and directly underneath the building's dome stands a larger than life statue of Abraham Lincoln, our country's sixteenth president. Mr. Lincoln was born in a cabin in Kentucky in 1809. Mr. Lincoln's statue shares the rotunda room with four other famous Kentuckians: Henry Clay, Alben Barkley, Dr. Ephraim McDowell, and Jefferson Davis—all men who played an important part in American history.

Alben Barkley served as vice-president under President Harry S. Truman. While in office, Mr. Barkley's grandson gave him the nickname "Veep." This nickname is still used for the vice president today.

Henry Clay served as a Senat U.S. Representative, and as Speaker of the House. He was also a three-time candidate for President.

Jefferson Davis was the President of the Confederate States during the Civil War. Strangely, at the only time the United States was divided, both the President of the Confederacy and the President of the Union were from Kentucky.

CLAY

Ephraim McDowell removed a 22.5-pound tumor from Jane Todd Crawford. Mrs. Crawford survived the surgery without anesthesia and was well enough to travel home on horseback in twenty-five days.

If you look at Mr. Lincoln's shoe, you'll notice it's shiny. That's because thousands of visitors have rubbed his toe for good luck.

r. Clay earned the ckname "The Great ompromiser" because his ability to help wmakers find some middle ound on the topic of slavery.

GREAT HALL

The Great Hall under construction in 1907.

After leaving the rotunda, take a flight of stairs and walk to one end of the capitol. You will truly see the vastness of the building. This incredible space is known as The Great Hall. The columns you see are Vermont granite. There are 36 altogether, each being 26 feet tall and weighing ten tons each. To ship them to the building site, each column had to be brought down the Kentucky River. Solid pieces such as these are no longer mined.

Above the Senate doors is a half circle picture. This is called a lunette. The lunette depicts Daniel Boone making a treaty, or agreement, with some Cherokee leaders. This treaty became known as the Treaty of Sycamore Shoals and allowed the settlers to purchase the land that we now know as Kentucky.

NOW THAT'S INTERESTING!!!

The stairs inside the capitol were modeled after the staircase at the Grand Opera House in Paris.

The rotunda is 7 stories high and was modeled after the rotunda above Napoleon's tomb.

The Gentleman from Kentucky

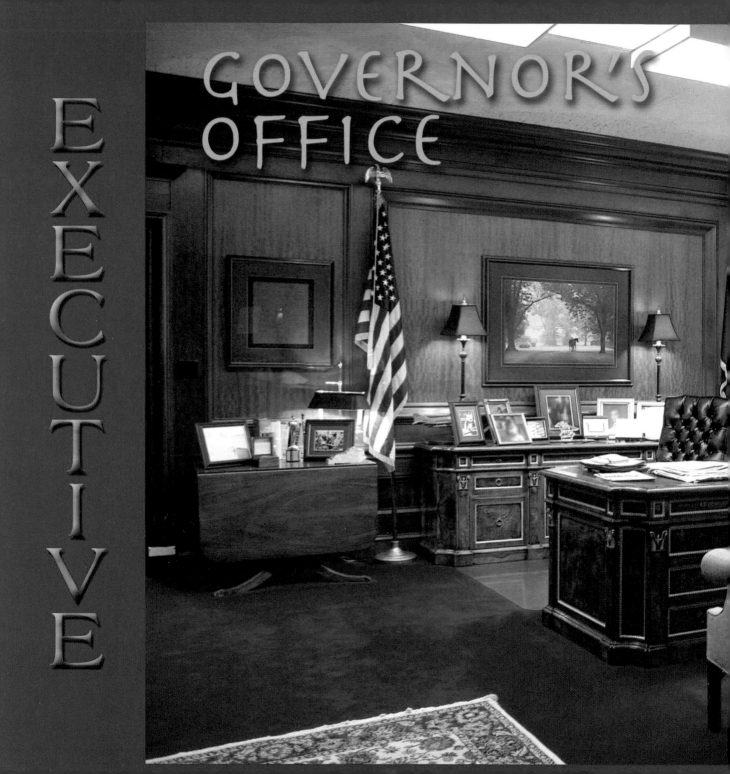

EXECUTIVE

GOVERNOR'S OFFICE

Straight behind the statue of Abraham Lincoln is the Kentucky Governor's Office. This is where the state's governor will work on making laws and decisions that will make Kentucky an even better place to live. He is a part of the **executive branch** of government —the part of government that helps to enforce the **laws**, or rules, that keep Kentuckians safe.

On the governor's office door is the state seal. Although the seal has changed over the years, this important state **symbol** now shows a well-dressed statesman shaking hands with a man in pioneer clothing. Above them is the **state motto:**

"United We Stand, Divided We Fall."

JUDICIAL

NOW
THAT'S INTERESTING!!!
You couldn't build the Supreme Court room again today. The Honduran mahogany is from the rain forest and is now illegal to log.
Kentucky is one of four commonwealth states in the U.S. Commonwealth actually means "Government for the good of all."
The Gentleman from Kentucky
EXIT

SUPREME COURT

Located on the second floor is the Kentucky Supreme Court. This is the highest court in Kentucky and makes up part of the **judicial branch** of government. The judicial branch, which includes all of Kentucky's courts, is responsible for interpreting the laws to make sure each one is fair.

The Supreme Court Chamber is the most expensive room in the entire capitol building. The wooden walls are made of mahogany that was shipped all the way from Honduras, and the marble came from Italy. Of course no ordinary light would do. This room's chandeliers are made of bronze.

In the front of the room sit seven chairs. These chairs are for the **justices**, or judges. These justices listen to cases and each one makes his or her own decision. Each justice is elected to serve for eight years and can then seek re-election. The chair in the middle is reserved for the Chief Justice, or main judge. Although there have been female justices, so far, all of Kentucky's Chief Justices have been men. Still, a female chief justice is sure to come. It may even be one of you!

LEGISLATIVE

HOUSE OF REPRESENTATIVES

On the top floor of the Capitol Building is the third branch in our government. It is called the **legislative branch.** This part of the government makes the laws. There are two chambers or groups of people who make up the legislative branch. One is the **House of Representatives**. The other is the **Senate**.

Young People in Government

You may be too young to vote for a representative or a senator, but you're not too young to play a part in Kentucky government.

Any citizen of any age can contact their legislators to express their opinions. You can write a letter, make a phone call, send an e-mail, or even meet the legislator in person.

You can also play another role. Kentucky children between the ages of 12 and 18 can serves as pages. A page is someone who runs errands for the legislators while they are debating bills. Pages aren't paid any money, but they do get to meet important officials and get a sneak peek at what's happening in Kentucky's government. If you would like to be a page, simply contact one of your state legislators.

SENATE

Kentucky's House of Representatives is made up of one hundred lawmakers that are elected every two years. Each lawmaker represents about 40,000 Kentucky voters. A representative's job is to help make laws that the citizens need and will support. This is often extremely difficult because the needs of some Kentuckians are not always the same as the needs of others. To help make decisions, the representatives must vote on a bill to see if it can go on to become a law. If a bill passes in the House of Representatives, it moves on to the Senate where it will be voted on and then sent to the governor.

The Kentucky Senate has only 38 members. The senators are elected every four years. Their job is much the same as those legislators in the House of Representatives—creating and voting on bills to become laws.

NOW THAT'S INTERESTING!!!

The state capitol building gets 75,000-80,000 visitors each year!

Many years ago, a legislator in the House of Representatives was not being heard. In an effort to get everyone's attention, he fired a pistol into the air, leaving a hole in the skylight.

The desks in the House of Representatives and Senate chambers are the original desks—over 100 years old!

The Senate is adorned with faux marble, called Scagliola, from Italy. Today it would be less expensive to use real marble!

The Gentleman from Kentucky

STATE RECEPTION ROOM

Also on the second floor is the gorgeous State Reception Room. Here the governor hosts formal parties like the one held the night before the Kentucky Derby. To make extra room for a large crowd, the windows along the wall open like doors. This leads to the terrace, so crowds can go easily in and out on a pretty day.

Don't try to move the center table! With its carved wood and marble top, the table alone weighs about 975 pounds! And those rugs on the walls aren't really cloth at all. They're oil paintings made to look like tapestries. Special artists must sometimes come in to touch them up if they get damaged.

Yet, most people find the mirrors to be the most fascinating part of the State Reception Room. These mirrors are modeled after the Hall of Mirrors in the Palace of Versailles in France. Because they face one another, they are reflecting each other's reflection. The reflection of each mirror bounces off the other again and again and again. This means you can look in one mirror and see a row of mirrors that never stops. Never! This is an example of infinity.

NOW THAT'S INTERESTING!!!

The State Reception Room was the governor's office until 1955. Until that time, the office contained a private stairway that led to an underground tunnel. This tunnel went to the governor's mansion and served as a quick escape in case of emergency.

A tour guide once discovered a live hawk in the State Reception Room. It's believed the creature was swept in through the large air ducts. Employees of the Department of Fish and Wildlife had to capture and release the bird.

The Gentleman from Kentucky

FIRST LADIES

Don't leave Kentucky's Capitol Building without stopping to view Kentucky's First Ladies in Miniature. It's true. But these aren't just any dolls. The **First Lady** is the hostess for important events and dinners. Most often it is the wife of the presiding governor. Occasionally the governor has not been married so a female relative has acted as the hostess. There is one big exception. Martha Layne Collins has been Kentucky's only female governor. She acted as governor and first lady at the same time.

Susannah Hart Shelby
1st and 5th First Lady
Wife of
Governor Isaac Shelby

Glossary

Capital—the town or city where lawmakers meet to discuss and vote on government issues.

Capitol—the building where lawmakers meet to discuss and vote on government issues.

Citizen—any person living within certain borders. All people who live in Kentucky are its citizens.

Executive branch—the part of government responsible for enforcing the laws.

First lady—the official hostess for state dinners and functions, usually the wife of the governor.

Frankfort—Kentucky's capital city.

House of Representatives—an elected group of 100 members who help create new laws. Each member serves a two-year term.

Inauguration—the ceremony in which the governor-elect takes the oath of office and officially becomes governor.

Judicial branch—the part of government responsible for interpreting the laws.

Justice—an elected official who serves on the Supreme Court.

Law—a rule created to help keep citizens safe or situations fair.

Legislative branch—the part of government responsible for creating laws.

Rotunda—a large room with a dome-shaped ceiling.

State motto—a phrase used to help describe the mind-set of citizens within the state. Kentucky's motto is "United We Stand, Divided We Fall."

Senate—an elected group of 38 members who help create new laws. Each member serves a four-year term.

Symbol—a picture or item that represents a group of people or a place.

IN MINIATURE

The Kentucky Federation of Women Clubs started the tradition of the dolls back in 1971. Each doll wears a small replica of the gown the First Lady wore to the **inauguration** ball. This ball takes place after the governor's official swearing in ceremony. Even the hair is made to resemble each First Lady. The display begins with Susannah Hart Shelby, wife of Kentucky's first governor, Isaac Shelby, and then moves all the way up to the present-day First Lady. This display, along with the building's many other special features, helps to make Kentucky's Capitol a unique place for visitors of all ages.

Martha Layne Hall Collins
Kentucky's First Woman Governor